CON
FRONT
ING YOUTH
APATHY

GREGG MOORE

Unless otherwise indicated, Bible quotations are taken from Life Application Bible – King James Version Tyndale House Publishers, Inc., Wheaton, Illinois, 1989, or Holy Bible – New Living Translation Second Edition Tyndale House Publishers, Inc., Carol Stream, Illinois, 2008.
www.publisher's website?

Any people depicted in stock imagery provided by Thinkstock are models, and such images are being used for illustrative purposes only. Certain stock imagery © Thinkstock.

Print information available on the last page.

Rev. date: 06/14/2016

To order additional copies of this book, contact:
Xlibris
1-888-795-4274
www.Xlibris.com
Orders@Xlibris.com
733590

Write the vision, and make it plain . . .
that (s)he may run that reads it.
—Habakkuk 2:2

To U.S. Bank manager, *Mr. Robert Muise,* particularly,
and to two managers *before* and *after* him,
Ms. Morgan Magistrate and *Ms. Alexa McCurdy.*

CONTENTS

Note: In this work, the sixty-six books of the Holy Bible are identified as numerals: Genesis as *1*, Revelation as *66*, Malachi as *39*, Matthew as *40*, etc.

{Back cover picture of Faith Oras at age 13 in Bar Beach in Victoria Island, Nigeria}

CONTENTS

INTRODUCTION

CONFRONTING YOUTH APATHY – without emotion, indifference

One wonders what the most important age in life is, and really, this is hard to say because so many societies and cultures exist with different ages being most important to each, so which one should we take as norm or standard? Alternatively, we could look at the most populous country in the world, India, and inquire what age is most important in that culture and then take that as an answer to our question. But two problems loom high; the first is that: is India really the most populous country on planet Earth since India is now two countries, Pakistan and India? So is half the original India or the India of today still the most populous country on earth? But the second issue is a problem that solves itself for this work is not about an age nor the importance of that age. Here, we are dealing with an age range and not a single age like twenty-one, forty, seventy, and lately the reigning age of sixty, not sixteen that one would have considered the most important at a time. Also, in considering age, our choice in this work is not because we think it is the most important age group—really, it could be—but because that is what we wish to concentrate upon, the adolescents, and again only just an aspect of that age group, *youth* and *apathy*, respectively or together.

On completion of my first book, *White Black and Other*, I gave a copy to my bank manager when I was last in his branch. But surprisingly, when I visited the branch again, Bob told me, "When you next write a book, can you write on youth apathy—how to deal with it?" His foremost concern in society was the problem of the youth, the supposed leaders of tomorrow, who are wasted by and large. This challenge was a bit surprising to me because he did not comment on the book he just bought dealing with race improvement in society, and neither could he have completely read it all, but the youth problem in American society was his problem, and I promised to take this up.

In this very first week of this year 2016, we all woke up to hear the shocking news of what happened last week in the Brownsville section of Brooklyn in New York, where five hooded men approached a man and his eighteen-year-old daughter in a Brooklyn playground operated by the New York City Park. One of the young men pointed a gun at the pair and ordered the father to leave. And after the father left the scene, the news continued, each of the males raped the eighteen-year-old girl. The hooded guys were found to be between the ages of fourteen and seventeen. Two were caught by the New York Police, and two turned themselves in, and one is still at large. Will anyone disagree with Bob, who, shortly after the purchase of a book, recommended or inquired if his next book could be on youth apathy? So, America and the world at large, I present to you *Confronting Youth Apathy*, which I dedicate to Bob. Happy reading.

CHAPTER 1

IT'S TIME FOR A CHANGE

Regarding leaders, be they company presidents, state governors, kings or queens, for example the Queen of England, or the president of a nation like ours, the United States of America, have we ever considered *what got them there*? Their birth, upbringing, youth, family circumstances, or education to name a few. This year 2016 is presidential-election year here in the United States, and it will be spectacular, however it turns out, just like that of Barack Obama's eight years ago, when a non-White erroneously styled the first black president, even though he is not **black** but *other*, reached out, ascended into and claimed the White House for the first time. The confusion is accentuated because even the president labels himself black when his children are not even black, the only black person in the first family being the first lady. But certainly not the president because he was gestated for 9 months and emanated into this world from a **white** womb.

So this year's presidential election will be most spectacular when America joins the list of nations like India already mentioned with a lady president. Mind you, I did not say a white lady. Even if Hillary Clinton doesn't win the presidency, I see no reason why the election of the most qualified for the office among the pack will equally be grandiose, especially since he is not a known politician and, for one reason or another known only to him, has chosen on a number of occasions not to be politically correct, more so that this candidate, Ben Carson, will be a truly black president. Talking about peculiarity, he is indeed a scholar, and have we not been told from time immemorial that the three foremost professions in the world are medicine, theology, and law? Should Hillary Clinton be president, it will not be because of her profession because several lawyers have been preseidents like the current president, and you don't need to go too far to get another lawyer. Just take away the president before Obama's predecessor and you get another lawyer. Her uniqueness as president will not be by profession nor by race but by gender, unlike Carson, a truly black man who will be unique in more than one way.

We are talking about leaders presently, what they could do and their upbringing. I want us to consider another; you might say a king of kings for he ruled 127 provinces or countries from India to Ethiopia: Xerxes also known as Ahasuerus. What do leaders do, one might wonder. They can do anything. This monarch had a mind-blowing party in the third year of his reign (17:1:2), and apart from the very distinguished set of invitees, his party celebrations lasted for over five months, for 180 days precisely. As if this was not enough, immediately after everyone returned to base with invitees coming from 127 countries, he threw another party for dignitaries in the state capital alone, even though this latter party was for only seven days when compared with the party of about six months nonstop, yet seven days of nonstop party is huge too! Do guests (and host) go home to take their baths and certainly not to eat anything since menu was surplus or in abundance and drinks too which had no limit (17:1:8). Could this celebrant have been a youth sometime in his life? Certainly.

Can any one remember Woodstock in 1969 – a Music and Art Fair that was held in Bethel New York and which attracted over 400, 000 people and whose wave echoed as far as West Africa and I guess beyond. That is the kind of things youths can do. But the Woodstock festival even went past the last day set for it, the 17th of August 1969! And even in Africa then and in High School, the waves of the New York festival rocked Lagos Nigeria especially among students in the elite institutions in particular *St Gregory's College Ikoyi Lagos*. If the New York Woodstock festival could make such waves around the world, can it be imagined what resonance this party by Xerxes a monarch would have made around the then known world when everything was in abundance and more than enough? Youths have energy and when means and wealth is also available to them in what they intend to do, the explosion could be terrific indeed. And in such situations so many youths could get wasted and some could pass out through drugs misunderstanding or violence, with the result that many of those that participated in those events are never the same any more. But could there be drunkenness, addiction, blood spill and or rape in such festivals? Certainly. But Woodstock was just a party even though it was replicated in other places around the world. And if we should consider just a single fallout or the ills that could occur at such parties like sex, even if it were not rape but consensual, the participants are no more what they were before that orgy, And this could have serious consequence for opportunities of later life as we shall soon see in this narration, because problems actually occurred at that party or at its extension when the reigning Queen refused the summoning orders of her Lord which led to a replacement contest being staged that required only two entry qualifications: beauty and virginity. So what would have happened to any girl who either by force, consent, willingly, allurance and/or by deception gave up and or lost her virginity. She automatically disqualified herself for the contest of the decade. But we should not jump there yet but continue step wisely until we reach the next chapter. The simple point being made here is that youth is a season in life like all others that is full of opportunities and pit falls, but may be much more than any other age group of life!

The partying was so special that the description of the decorations and venue arrangement was second to none (17:1:7). Even the queen, who also must have had a spectacular upbringing too as we shall soon see, had her own party too. But luck fell against her, some will say, because that celebration spelled her doom, which possibly was a plan and so should not be seen as her doom or demise, even though she did leave office. I mean, stopped from being queen as a result of her orchestration and/or planning. On the last day of this shorter festivity, the king, we were told, was in high spirits and sent for the queen so as to display her beauty to the mammoth crowd of the invitees. But the queen, on her own volition, refused to honor the king with her presence. Why, you may wonder, or was there a feud between the king and queen at the time? Maybe but highly unlikely since the king was in high spirits, we were told. It appeared, it may be suggested, that the queen wanted to pass her position as queen to her friend or companion, the second runner-up in the competition that got her the first-lady position. But do we need to jump the gun to arrive at this explanation? Not at all, for in the next chapter, we shall delve further into this. With the vacuum created in the kingdom, without a queen in the palace, a replacement mechanism was set into motion, unfortunately not as the queen and her companion had envisaged.

The king, like the right leader that he was, consulted with the members of his cabinet for not exactly a replacement of a queen but a solution of the matter at hand of a queen refusing to honor the king with her presence when summoned to do so that everything be done according to law in a pre-democratic society, which tells us how great the society was and its king. Two suggestions eventually emerged, one from the supreme cabinet and the other lower council, which eventually turned out to be the ratified and adopted suggestion. Senate member Memucan, may be the senate president or voice, no one knows, had, in brief, suggested that another queen, next in command or runner-up queen, who invariably must have come second in the beauty contest that got the deposed Vashti to the throne and now her companion or "running mate" if I may use that terminology, be enthroned, just as Vashti herself had anticipated. Also, an edict that *the man should be ruler in his own house and do whatever he pleases* (17:1:22) was enacted.

CHAPTER 2

IN A DEMOCRACY, WHO RULES: THE LOWER HOUSE, THE SENATE, OR THE PEOPLE?

In solving an important matter in the state at that time, it was the opinion of the lower house, the House of Representatives one might say that eventually carried the day, overriding that which was propounded/proposed by the Senate. And because, on many occasions, things from the top are not usually speedily executed and should there be perceived or actual vacuum or gap that needs to be filled, emergency workable alternative do arise, which, indeed, may be the plan of God. In the Xerxes kingdom, we were told (i) as the king's anger subsided, (ii) he began thinking about the deposed queen which leads to the theory that there was no love lost before the queen's act of disobedience. (iii) With the deposed queen's plight and the decree in force ensuring the non reversal of her punishment of being permanently removed as queen, the king's personal attendants, whom I called the lower house earlier (since houses essentially make laws), counterproposed that (a) the entire empire of 127 provinces be thoroughly searched for young virgins, (b) agents be dispersed throughout the empire to bring the selected beautiful young women to a special section of the palace where beauty treatments would be administered to them, and (c) a final contest for the next queen be staged. As a result of the appeal to this latter proposal, even though originating from lower officers in government, it was accepted by the monarch and automatically put it into motion.

That is when our heroine came into the picture. She was a youth, at most in her middle adolescence: fourteen, fifteen or sixteen at the most. She was an orphan, no surviving parents, which could be a cause for being apathetic and losing her way in life by joining bad age-group gangs; getting wayward; getting hooked on drugs, gambling, smoking, and other vices the youth are guilty of today or at any time in history; getting involved in sex, stealing, and the list goes on. But she had an older cousin who adopted her. Though this appeared a stopgap against disaster, the girl could still have been wayward and then go on to blame her waywardness to the loss of her real parents in early years, which no one wished for, not even for one's enemies, as reasons for apathy, which is so common among our youth today even with actual parents around and often with available amenities too. Though a sizable youth apathy and falling by the wayside is largely due to poverty, and recently in America due to wealth too *Re. the Affluenza youth* with the full support of his mother, both nabbed in Mexico after Christmas last year 2015 who both might still be in jail right now as this work goes to print! But Esther, also Hadassah, for so was she called, turned out really great, for her guardian would not have spared spanking her, despite their closeness, so as to bring out the best in her. Who should get the credit for Esther's greatness, therefore: her cousin turned father and guardian, Mordecai, who probably spanked her when she transgressed, or her very self that did not run to the police to make a report when spanked? Or could it be her dead parents, who did a great work, starting the spanking in the very short time they had with the baby girl Hadassah so that when cousin Mordecai continued in the same vein, this was not alien to the girl?

Looking at this very example, I think both cousins did very well, so therefore, the answer to the question in the above paragraph is not an either-or situation and neither is it an all-or-none. It is an all-of-the-above situation.

Now let us, for a moment, picture how a healthy home should be. We all agree there should be discipline as corrections for wrongdoing, though the definition of discipline the world over, even here in the heartland of America, differs. Maybe the law in all fifty states rejects spanking, forgetting (or is it not knowing) what the Bible says in (20:13:24): He that spares his rod hates his child. No much surprise, though, when recently, the highest court in the land ruled gay marriage as right in all fifty states, something which in-whom-we-trust detests (3:18:22). That is, however, not our concern here, which is that how did they live in the family of Mordecai? Girls will always be girls, and boys will always be boys, it is often said, but one seldom hears that said of fathers, yet good fathers have existed through the ages, and so good fathers will always be good. So we can picture Esther jumping up to hug her guardian-father or sitting on his lap during bedtime stories or going on an errand or even crying not because she remembered her dead parents—because I am sure Mordecai did not give room for that—but because she was disciplined for a wrong she had done, a pruning process to bring out the best in her, not to abuse her or dehumanize her as politically correct America would think. Even though, much later, Dr. Benjamin Spock later told America we shouldn't spank our children when they misbehave because, as he put it, their little personalities would be warped and we might damage their self-esteem, too bad, his son committed suicide. And because we say an expert should know what he's talking about, even if this is against the Bible, as this issue of spanking children who offend is, we say it is okay for the son of Dr. Benjamin Spock to commit suicide. So best in behavior Esther turned out to be at last. Almost forgot to mention that as obedient as she was and very-good-mannered too, she was surprisingly stunningly beautiful too. And we would not know of this if not for the agents sent out because of the edict from the lower house. They nabbed her and took her—an adolescent—to the palace, to the house of women.

And so the tie of the close-knit family was broken. What happens to most of our youth when they go away from home and get into groups like those in the university, where they work (study), play, eat, live, sleep, and wake up away from loved ones? Although I graduated from high school in mid teens, I did not enter the university until my early twenties, precisely at twenty-two; but in both, I lived away from home, in a boarding house and a hall of residence. Maybe we should ask somebody to tell us what kids do in both places away from home. Oh no, we shouldn't go there at all, for even while at home with parents, we still have teen pregnancies, drug addiction, cigarette smoking, or even suicide. There is a myriad of vices the youth get themselves into, especially when they leave home, but not so with Esther. Among other girls with total freedom, we are told she still continued to obey her guardian-father just as if she was still under him (17:2:10). True enough, Mordecai attempted to continue the supervision and guidance of Esther when she was in the palace before the contest, but was he able to? The answer is yes and no. *No*, because Mordecai couldn't enter the palace, especially into the place where the contestants young virgins, one of which will be the next queen of the land, were nurtured. So all he could do was one of the things he had thought her daughter-cousin to do while still under his roof, the prayer-walk (17:2:11), and so the answer is *yes* too.

How did Esther fare in the harem? One word: distinguishable. You can imagine the mind-set of a youth still in her virginity and who is not loose or loud with the prospect of becoming the next Queen or First Lady in the nation, how she would carry herself. It was even said they were given special treatment in body, hair, food, and clothing. They could get whatever they wished for or demanded, especially when it is their turn for the contest and be brought before the monarch. But through all these steps, Hadassah-Esther distinguished herself before all and sundry—a prime example of a youth that did not lose it at any level. But does that automatically make her the coveted winner of the crown? By no means, though it puts her in a good position to go for it and get it. And because of the good training she got from home, which could not be hidden but displayed, the chief coach and Director Hegai, became a second father to Esther while away from home for a contest whose training took years, even maybe equal to, if not more than, the years for obtaining a regular four-year degree. Esther listened to elders' advice, took nothing extra that was not recommended to her for her contest by her guardian-coach Hegai, and emerged queen in place of Vashti (17:2:17).

Before we leave this topic, can you consider the number of eligible spinsters, all virgins, that were in this contest for the office of queen of a vast expanse of land that is said to embrace 127 previously independent nation-states that stretched from India to Ethiopia?

We started this theme in the previous chapter let us continue it here now. Esther had a very good upbringing and was beautiful. She has been selected to compete for the position of the next Queen in this gigantic kingdom. But what if some serious occurrences had happened to her, call it mistake, not at all her fault or whatever but which her cousin-uncle did not know about despite the very good training she received. I say this because teenagers in particular know how to hide things away from their parents: be it cigarette smoking, experimentation with drugs including sex and the initial stages of teen pregnancy? The contest mentioned in the previous chapter is now here; which contest if we remember has only two qualifications: to be extremely **beautiful** and to be a **virgin**. Oh how many girls have lost their virginity at a time they did not expect it, like the rail car or alley rape of females both of mothers and children. But our concern here is teen rape which automatically disqualifies a good girl from such a contest. As I write this I remember an incidence that took place in my very presence, and too bad and so unfortunately, I couldn't be of much or any assistance to the rape victim. The year was 1969 or 1970, I guess in the latter. This teen age in her vacation period had met a young man in his early 20's that became her boyfriend. She was full of dreams of a very bright future with her boyfriend who treated her very ladylike and respectably. She was about to return to a coed boarding high school in another city and state where she would now solely concentrate on her studies and wish for another holiday, when she would come meet her working boyfriend in her home city and state. So before she traveled back to school, she came in to say hi to her boyfriend which unfortunately was not back from work, may be he stopped to see a boyfriend after work which actually came home with him on that fateful day. But on this girl's arrival, she was locked in her boyfriend's room by another male, older than her but younger than her boyfriend who then either tore or soaked her pants or entire dress in water to prevent her from escaping naked who then called in his friend and both now raped this girl in turn. Her dress was then ironed dried and was then released. When her actual boyfriend arrived from work with his friend, ego narrated what he witnessed to the boyfriend who too might have bragged to his friend about his new girlfriend. He then called ego aside and drilled him on what to say. And in the presence of his friend asked ego: which Edna were you talking about, was she Edna X and ego responded no Sir but Edna Y but the friend was not fooled, he plainly saw the cover up and that incidence ended the friendship relation between this teenage girl and her new found boyfriend who later went to Hamburg, West Germany to study medicine and returned to Nigeria with his white wife and two sons! What if Esther too was raped in one of those occasions she was out either on errand or just went to say hello to a friend as Edna did and met with disaster. Then no matter the prayer walk of Mordecai, during the beauty contest, Esther could never have become the next Queen and the chance to save the Jews would have been lost, at least through her.

We should also remember that people were not told to apply, as we do for jobs this day, but agents were sent out throughout the length and breadth of a vast empire to search for a replacement queen, which most probably the people did not know what these officials were looking for. Certainly, they were not talking to boys, so it could not have been for enlistment in the army. But why girl? Most likely, it had been done before, at the death of a queen, or was it at the coronation of a new king? But many, if not virtually all, know there was a current queen in the land, so why this mass gathering of extremely beautiful young virgin girls with pleasant bodily features? If you know this man Mordecai, Esther's father, you can imagine how he must have felt when his adopted daughter was snatched from him without his permission and maybe without an explanation too.

Let us now fast-forward to the time when the last batch came in, for all agents must have gone in different directions to different regions of this vast empire on an identical assignment. Yes, when all these girls were gathered together and eventually told why they were primarily chosen and that one of them, out of may be hundreds or even thousands, will be the next queen and that Queen Vashti had been deposed. And for Esther to have emerged the winner, we heard, when it was Esther's turn to go to the king, Esther was taken to the king, Xerxes, at the royal palace in early winter (December–January) in the seventh year of his reign, meaning this marriage contest had been in orchestration for four solid years now since Vashti's removal. And the king loved Esther more than any of the other young women. He was so delighted in her that he set the royal crown on her head and declared her queen instead of Vashti (17:2:15–17).

Can an apathetic youth win such a trophy? What a joy it is when the youths are not apathetic but full of life and go out winning trophies and bringing them back to their parents and communities. This is presidential election year in America and as the title of this chapter reads in part **In a democracy, who rules:...,** will it not be appropriate at this junction to ask who occupies the White house next January: Will it be the Foxes or the Lions, by this I actually refer to a Sociological theory by that name propounded by an Italian, Vilfredo Pareto that stipulated that political power changes intermittently alternating between the foxes and the lions, that is, between the Democrats and Republicans. So who really will be America's President in less than a year. Will the person be a Republican to prove that Italian theorist right since a Democratic president Obama will be completing his second term of a cumulative 8 year presidency in less than 8 months or will another Democrat occupy the White house to invalidate the Parentian theory of the Foxes and the Lions? The race has been long and should we say interested and infused with partial surprises with the Republican Party having 17 candidates at the start of the Primaries and the Demo candidates being much fewer. Also both parties had at least one female presidential aspirants. And so the question could be asked: Will the next President be a male or for the very first time will she be a female? The race narrowed to 3 among the republican with a candidate Donald Trump winning more primaries than any other including his closest rival Ted Cruz. But as for the Democrats after a third candidate, a state governor fell off the wagon the race has been vigorously fought between pure Democrat Hillary Clinton – a female and a Democratic Socialist (or is he Social Democrat) Bernie Sanders which although Hillary according to poll results has a lead over Sanders but the game is still anybody's of the two. And so in the next term, who rules Republican or still Democrats, and as usual a male or will it be a female this time around for the first time in the greatest or should we say the most sophisticated democracy on planet earth?

The king celebrated Esther's coronation with a great banquet for all his nobles and officials, even declaring a public holiday for the provinces and giving generous gifts to everyone (17:2:18). Wow! Although Esther was now next to the king and so very powerful in the land, it was said that she still continued to honor her father and mother (so that her days may be long in the land God had made her queen (2:20:12)). She even secured a palace appointment for her guardian-father that provided a multiplier effect. Her family of orientation was close to her again, and the king's life was saved from an assassination attempt only because her guardian-father on duty heard about the assassination plot by some disgruntled palace officials (17:2:21–22), who most probably were loyal to the deposed queen Vashti and her companion, for whom she rebelled against and refused to go to the king on the last day of the seven-day minor celebration so as to make room for her partner too to play queen as probably planned by both. But as a result of the counter-edict which emanated from the lower house, the original plan of the first and second most beautiful ladies in the original contest for the queen of the land was aborted (17:1:19). The report of the attempted royal assassination was found to be authentic and confirmed, and judgment was served on the culprits, but shouldn't there be a compensation, a promotion for the man that uncovered this diabolical plot to murder the king? Answer: We shall soon see. Whatever happens at the end of the day, it is good to remember as in 19:75:6-7 that says: *For promotion cometh neither from the east, nor from the west, nor from the south. But God is is the judge: he putteth down one, and setteth up another.*

CHAPTER 3

STOCHASTIC LIFE OCCURRENCES: ARE YOU READY FOR THE ONE THAT IS ABOUT TO HIT YOU?

What do you think about, or do you know what happens in the world every day? Or should I ask an easier and more straightforward question: How can we know everything that happens in the world? The thinking aspect of the question is redundant since we don't have to think—we just watch or listen to the news. And so in a part of the world, the leading part of the world at that very time, and from the world's capital city, Susa, emanated a mind-boggling news that a single man, who was a relatively unknown government official, had been promoted above everybody. Did you get what I just said? Above everybody, even the seven men in the supreme council who knew the law and without whom the king dare not, or should I say the king would not dare, take any action, major or minor. There is always a first time, some say, but the point being made here is that it was documented (17:1:13), and if it was documented that the king always asked advice from his supreme council because they knew all the Persian laws and customs, then we have an exception. Why is it that he did not consult them before setting up the hitherto relatively unknown Haman over everyone else? I think I can venture an answer, but maybe not now. Let's just go on.

So it was announced sometime after the new queen was installed, maybe two years later, that a new office has been created, that of the prime minister, and the first occupier of that position will be the relatively unknown Haman. In addition to the selected officer for this newly created position being relatively unknown just as the reason for the creation of this office not also clear, but equally puzzling was why the Office of Prime Minister did not go to one of the **first 7** in the kingdom, the Supreme Council - may be to that member who proposed a solution to the problem on hand at the time when the king's order was disregarded and disobeyed by no less a subject as the queen, I mean to minister Memucan. And the additional news or information was that all around the palace should bow to this newly appointed prime minister whenever he is spotted. (Can anyone see a similarity between this and an edict of another ancient world power in Babylon that involved three youth: Shadrach Meshach and Abednego (27:3:19–20))?

It all started around the palace, but guess what, it would soon flow out from just among palace officials unto others in the capital and then to the extreme parts of the 127 provinces or independent nation-states, from India to Ethiopia, that made up the Persian kingdom of King Xerxes. How did this edict arise, and what could be the underlying force? We shall all tackle this two-in-one mystery question together very soon. After all, did I not say I will come back to this soon? But for now, we could take as a given without proof that the source of both mysteries is one and the same. Why a man from nowhere should ascend to a position hitherto unknown, and why all should bow when they see him? Do subjects even bow to their king just on sighting him even when afar off and not when in his presence on a business as a form of honor and salutation? But the unfolding of this mystery is not far-fetched, which we shall soon see. Do we remember the one that told God's own son at the commencement of his earthly ministry to bow before him in exchange of giving God's son what he came into this world to do, human redemption and salvation, and that without going by way of the cross?

So many, if not all, people bowed whenever this mystery man, I almost said a magician, was around; but there was one who did not do this. He most probably remembered three others referenced two paragraphs above and the written law of God (2:20:5). So

Prime Minister Haman not only decided to kill this rebel of a man, whose religion would not permit him to bow to a human being, but he additionally decided to blot out from the surface of the earth all other people that believe as this man believed; and by crook and means, he once again got the king to sign an edict to destroy the entire race and people of a man whose religion was more than just a lip service to the deity he believed in.

Let us, for a minute, consider the scenario before us right now. Because somebody refused to bow before a man, that person must not only die, but all his people and race must die too, even if they never saw this culprit, heard about him, nor are related to him in any way. How did this satanic individual pull this through?

Maybe that is not a relevant question to consider now, but that a whole race must be wiped out because a man, one of them decided to obey God rather than man certainly is. And so there was wailing and crying everywhere throughout the entire empire, for a date had been set for the mass murder of a whole race of good and holy people, which date would be sometime in the following year. As this wicked and unrighteous decree was issued as law and publicized throughout the entire land for all peoples to get ready to do their duty against a particular people which was *to kill, cause to perish and to take the spoil of them for a prey* – that is, to loot. Yet some rejoiced as others rejoiced **alongside those rejoicing** because as we were told *the enemy could not countervail the king's damage* (17:3:15). But when imminent danger looms high and certain, apart from mass weeping and wailing as well as trepidation and fear, is there anything more the people of God can do or should do? Are they just to fold their arms and await the inevitable? Certainly, faith should rise high, and the believer should look up to God who never fails to respond at such times. For a thought unto possible answers in such scenarios, what did Moses do for the Israelites at the Red Sea with the Egyptian host behind them (2:14:15–16) or, again, what did the people of Jabesh-Gilead do in another situation when enemy Ammonites with their king Nahash came to humiliate the Israelites (9:11:3)?

Is there anything more people can do apart of mass weeping and wailing as well as trepidation and fear when imminent danger looms high and certain is what we are discussing right now. We shall now give more examples of how people of faith through the years have handled the situation:- once with a decree in force that no human being should say prayer or supplication to any god or Idol but only to the monarch, and that doing that was at the risk of that person's life, as no matter who he or she is would be fed to hungry lions in an ancient kingdom. And no less than the Prime minister himself who happened to be a believer in the Almighty God, damned all consequences opened his window to face Jerusalem and prayed normally despite what the members of his household might have feared and may be persuaded him into suspending his prayer for that short period time while the embargo lasted. He was thrown to the lions but the lions automatically became pets and endured further starvation for one more day until these were fed by the flesh of not one but many more human beings (Dan 6).

What about when a plot to assassinate a world preacher was announced by a Word of Prophesy which was announced at a religious gathering and all pleaded with that man of God not to go to the place he had planned to visit as he was going to be killed. But all he said was that *why do you weep to break my heart, that I am ready not only to be imprisoned but to die for the cause of Christ and his gospel.* And when things began to unfold, it so happened that the God that this man served spoke out and said: *Be encouraged Paul. Just as you have been a witness to me here in Jerusalem, you must preach in Rome as well (Acts 23:11),* and so he did not die. Even Jesus after he had been sold for 30 pieces of Silver and arrested in the Garden of Gethsemane told the officers that arrested him: *if it is me that you seek, let these all go.* And just in the next chapter 4 of this book, we shall hear what a female teen said that has become may be the most important verse in the Bible Esther 4:16, as important as John 3:16 if not more important!

CHAPTER 4

FASTING: OF WHAT USE IS IT IN LIFE?

In this section, we want to try and address *three* questions at the least: What is the fundamental cause of youth apathy? Why is it rampant? And is there any hope of it abating? We shall also be considering how to resolve the misunderstanding that results from the youth-elders age gap. And most importantly, we shall be considering something that is not spoken about in most circles, and even where, say, lip service is given to it as an age-old tradition, we don't know what it really means and or what it can do and not do. I mean, the liturgy of fasting. So starting with three questions, we now have five.

As people of God, what should be our attitude when we disagree with fellow believers? Should loved ones fight, quarrel, and/or disagree in the process of tackling the same problem? When there is a disagreement between brethren, does this mean at all times that one is right and the other wrong, or could there be a need of a meeting of minds to find a way out to solve the same problem?

And so a decree had been promulgated that an entire race—not just any race but the first race on earth, the race that emanated from a man who actually was the grandson of another man simply described as the *friend of God* (14:20:7)—would be annihilated. So what did this man who disobeyed the law of the land do when he heard about the decree on the consequence of his actions? We are told he (1) tore his clothes and put on burlap and ashes, (2) went out into the city, crying with a loud and bitter wail, and (3) even went as far as the palace gate, which is forbidden for any

---

man to do. This man, we may note, was always doing what was forbidden for a man to do. First and foremost, all men should bow to the prime minister-god.; he didn't, which caused serious problems. And now, in attempting to solve the problem, he again did another thing that no man was allowed to do: going as far as the palace gate in rag or mourning clothes. His action set the example for his people everywhere. What type of example do you set for people everywhere you go to, friend? In the process, the news reached everywhere, including the palace, where rumors do not fly very easily. Or how can one coup then another coup of military takeover in rotten and corrupt African democracies occur when the people in government and at the helm of affairs don't know this until it happens? So the news got to the palace that a half-naked man was at the gate, and surprisingly, it hit target—obviously, the king did not know this, but the queen was informed. But how could she have been informed when she was instructed by her guardian-father that she should not disclose her identity under any circumstances? And like the awesome youth that she was, though now a queen, she still obeyed and respected Mordecai who commanded that she kept her origin a secret.

In first informing the queen, I sometimes wonder if this was merely done to get the information fast to the king since his queen is, or should be, closest to the king, but if this was the reasoning of the palace staff that first informed the queen about the naked man in the palace gate, and later of the naked man himself to the same, their calculation was so very wrong because on informing the queen, she even avoided to tell her husband about this at all, and even when she agreed to do so, she took all the time, and when she agreed to do this, she did so passing through the long route, merry-go-round some will say. Or could it be that the queen was first approached with the unusual news because it had been suspected that there was something unexplainable between the queen and this naked man since it had been observed that the queen and this now naked or probably crazy man regularly meet at a spot and unfailingly without an intermediary.

Someone else apart from the palace officials, as just mentioned above, also received a shocker because he too thought the queen was the shortest route to the king, but surprisingly, he was dead right at last, which again came through dialogue with a youth. The point being made is that parents and guardians have a responsibility to train, and possibly spank the child in the process of training, in his or her formative years, which will then form a reference point when the going gets tough, storms of life, some call it; because then, as it is said, when the going gets tough, it is the tough that gets going.

What authority or reference point do we have for not disciplining a child? I must admit there is a learning style that is accredited, maybe accepted, worldwide that simply states that a child should do whatever he or she wants or likes to do and should just be watched—the Monticello. Not sure these know there is a devil out there that can enter into humans and can make them do things they may later regret and possibly kill themselves for doing, if and when it seemed too late to retrace their steps. But the better way is to train a child by discipline if need be, whether woman-to-woman, Naomi and Ruth; woman-to-man, Hannah and Samuel; man-to-woman, Mordecai and Esther; or man-to-man, Paul and Timothy, for instance, for the parent to tell the child *stay there*, etc. It is, therefore, not surprising that Esther could always come out to meet Mordecai at a certain exact time he previously told her without needing the services of a go-between to tell Esther "That man is here for you again." But an emergency occurred after their last meeting. How then can Mordecai communicate with Queen Esther or get her attention? You just hold on.

In 1 Timothy 1:3, it says, "Let no man despise thy youth." This training has to do with an individual not viewing achievement or attaining goals as beyond the reach of the youth, a fact that makes so many youth lose it and/or take vices like drugs and alcohol, including smoking marijuana or even mere cigarette and committing crimes such as rape, which all are unnecessary and bad.

In 1 Timothy 4:12, it says, "Do not lay hands unadvisedly on anybody." This simply warns that we should not do things hastily like youths do, but we should always think it through before taking action. But some adults fail here too, only because they didn't learn it right as youth. Or else, why should they fail now since what you are trained in stays with you for life?

I Tim 5:22 and **teach this things** I Tim 6:2. Oh, but many never learn these right things nor teach the right things like knowing that *godliness with contentment is great gain. For we brought nothing into this world, and it is certain we can carry nothing out* (54:6:7-8); *...man....flee these things* I Tim 6:11; *fight the good fight....* (54:6:12).

So it then happened that the scene being created by the secret and unknown may be nighttime visitor to the queen—an abomination or, if you prefer, and unlawful act of walking in rags or naked near and into the gate of the "White House" was reported to the first lady who quickly sent raiment to cover up the nakedness of this unknown special visitor the queen usually come out to meet, because, mind you, Queen Esther is under instruction not to divulge the secret of her race or family. And to make things worse, the man refused to take the royal apparels. The teenage queen must have been really confused, and if you were the one—oh, I am sorry. If your daughter was the one in such a predicament, what will you advise her to do or what will she do as in this case without an adviser? Lose it, take a bottle of beer or wine, light a cigarette, or go into her private toilet to take a wrap of weed? But not Esther who had learned from infancy to shun youthful apathy. So she summoned a court official and said to him, "Go and ask that man what the matter is?"

And so Mordecai related to Esther through an intermediary (17:4:7–8) *all that had happened unto him and of the sum of money Haman, the prime minister, had promised to pay the king's treasuries to destroy the Jews. He also gave the palace official a written copy of the decree to destroy them, which was given at the capital, to show and declare it unto Esther and to charge her that she should go unto the king and make supplication and request before him for her people,* which until this moment, this man had told Esther to keep secret. The ensuing dialogue between this adolescent and her father was not funny. Let us see how it continued.

The court official was a very faithful messenger who ensured that he passed on the message he has been sent clearly and accurately from A to B and back again without addition, subtraction, or alteration. Taking Esther as A and Mordecai as B, let's go.

A: (tell him) whosoever, whether man or woman, shall come in unto the king into the inner court, who is not called, there is one law of his to put (that person) to death (whoever he or she may be), except such to whom the king shall hold out the golden scepter, that he may live: but I have not been called to come in unto the king these thirty days.

When this message was delivered to the guardian-father, he invariably said,

B: Are you arguing with me or giving excuses? What are you thinking? Do you think that you will escape more than the other Jews not living in the palace as you? Just go and do what I told you to do. But if you dare disobey me, the Jews will get help from unexpected quarters, and you and the Jews with you in the palace shall be destroyed, and who knows whether your being crowned as the queen of the empire was for a time as this?

Is that how anybody talks to the first lady of the land, whoever he may be? But that is only our minor concern; what this book is all about is just about to unfold. How the queen took this threat from her father figure is our main and only concern at this point. What should she do? What will a typical youth do or say? Tell him to go to hell, maybe, but oh no, not Esther.

This was her ready-made reply to her father, whom she probably left in the ghettos to now live in the palace as queen:

Go, gather together all the Jews that are present in (the capital), and fast ye for me, and neither eat nor drink, three days, night or day: I also and my maidens will fast likewise, and so will I go in unto the king which is not according to the law; and if I perish I perish (17:4:16).

What do you think this response meant, and what reaction did it exude from a father who hitherto had been a hard-liner that his orders should be obeyed, queen or no queen? What we were told is this: On hearing the above words, it was said that Mordecai went his way, and he did *according* (I would have said *exactly* if I were the narrator) to all that Esther had asked of him. For Mordecai was such a reasonable man who would take a keen look at a suggestion and consider the proposal even if coming from an opponent in a debate or argument.

So let us talk a little about fasting now, shall we?

Anything that you cannot achieve in any other way will yield and give way if you fast. Fasting is also prayer, but it is the extreme of prayer. A complete day's fast is food and water abstinence for twenty-four hours, for two is forty-eight hours, etc. Fasting, though mysterious, is God-ordained, not by man or Satan, and its dynamics is only known to God and to him alone, not man or Satan.

One need not fast, especially on medical grounds and maybe on that ground only. Other forms of fasting exist too like, during the duration of the fast, taking water alone, eating meals that are not full course, eating every night only, or just skipping breakfast. Fasting should always be accompanied with prayer for a specific cause, whatever it is. Fasting should also be accompanied with reading of some sections of the word of God, and be careful when you fast because the result can blow your mind. Jesus fasted, Moses fasted, Daniel fasted, Elijah fasted, Hannah fasted: the first two Jesus and Moses for 40 days each, even the second twice 40 for breaking God's letter engraved on stones to man on how he should live on earth. May be Moses broke the rock tablets for a good reason – for the people he brought out of slavery in Egypt had committed the believers' suicide, - which is lack of faith -by wanting to go back there to Egypt again. Since they were in the wilderness - for they said: as for the Moses we don't know where he is. Esther fasted but did Joseph, the eleventh son of Israel and Prime Minister in Egypt fast too? Maybe, maybe not—not sure if he did. But after the general's wife lied about what Joseph did to her and before Potiphar arrived, hours, days, or even a week, was he fed? Just asking. And generally, three days and three nights is the standard for beginners. One more example to buttress this— one of people who fasted for three days continuously is Saul. In 44:9:9, we read, "And he was three days without sight, and neither did eat or drink." But anytime you cannot continue, it is time to end it, for dying from fasting is a sin. But do you know some actually fasted until the fourteenth day, 276 people in all, when death at sea was imminent, until counseled by one of them to eat something? "And while the day was coming on, Paul besought them all to take meat, saying, 'This is the fourteenth day that ye have tarried and continued *fasting* having taken nothing . . .' Then were they all of good cheer, and they also took some meat" (44:27:33–36).

CHAPTER 5
THE TABLE TURNS AGAIN

I am of the belief that you can start reading a book from any chapter, and provided the entire book is eventually read, it will make complete sense to the reader eventually. This is more true in some cases than others, but should you have completed pre med courses or engineering or pharmacy, in which physics is taught, you would have known that the instructor could begin with any energy and, usually, if more than an instructor these could take different aspects simultaneously. But for this book. It is advised not to begin with chapter 5 without reading the previous chapters, in particular chapter 4, or just the last page of the last chapter before reading this chapter. But before we continue, can we refer back to the deposed Queen Vashti?

She was probably bitter about the fact that the king could call her whenever he so chooses, but she could not do the same but could only access the king at any time at the risk of her life. So she decided not to go to the king when he sent for her for reasons stated elsewhere in this book, a pact she made with her runner-up queen and not just to be defiant or being a forerunner of the women's liberation movement, which some have ventured to say emanates from the pit of hell and to which I do not think is completely wrong if at all. The gravity of the offense of the queen's refusal to go to the king when summoned falls squarely within the mores and norms of societies, which is slightly different from one society to another, with each society being lord of its own laws. But there are giant societies like that of the 127 provinces King Xerxes reigned over that took orders from a central government in Susa, the capital. I am sure the women liberation movement would have been strong, had it existed then, in support of the deposed Queen Vashti, though, unfortunately, could not have helped restore her to monarchy. Something happened though; women are still powerful, for the case in question, the monarch could have been very easily ousted for removing a queen, whatever her fault might be, especially refusing to answer a man's call when summoned—mind you, not any man but her royal spouse—if not for Mordecai, the cousin, the new youth queen who uncovered the assassination of the king (17:2:22).

But there is a way, a method, that delivers all the time and without fail. If really so, why don't people rush that way, one might ask. Maybe because it too has its requirements for it to work, for it might be painful to the body, resulting to body weakness, hunger pangs, thirst, dryness of lips, inability of the individual to do his or her regular activities and the requirement to talk to God and to present yourself to God to talk to you too. There is a factor that is crucial too that may pull humans from this method that guarantees achievement but not sure to what extent, which is the requirement of a holy life or living. But by commencing with confession of sins and a willingness and determination to live clean ever after, though the individual may still fall, that could easily be taken care of. And lest I forget another factor that stands alone, the factor of faith—exercising it. But regarding fasting, it was established that this one goeth not out but by prayer and fasting. Really of fasting and faith, it is hard to say which is more important, for both guarantee results. Was it not said elsewhere that if you have faith as small as a grain of mustard seed, you could tell a mountain to be removed from its position and go into the sea and remain there, and it will be so (40:17:20)? But by and large, presumption is taken for faith unknowingly by many, but you cannot do something else and mistakenly take it for fasting, for according to this youth queen, it should be night and day of no food, not even water. When you are doing that, you are in a fast, provided, of course, you tell God why you are doing that and hear him (read his word) also at such a time. Otherwise, it might just be a hunger strike, which really is not directed to God but to man, whether in authority or just any human whose attention the subject seeks.

But before the fast was actually over, we are told that on the third day—67 percent of the fast already gone but still in it, racing to finish the 33 percent remaining—this fasting woman—young lady, I should say, not sure now if she was even twenty yet, but she could be— ventured to approach the king, which hitherto she knew was wrong to do without being summoned by the monarch. She even had told someone seeking her assistance to get a request that is impossible to do or had never been done across to the king. On that date, while the group fast was still on, she put on her royal robe, dressing so nicely and putting on something more, which others in the fasting group really didn't need, especially now since they were in their respective homes and were not required to risk their lives going to the king uninvited—she put on *faith* too. I suppose those at home will also need this, even though they certainly will not be killed for praying and fasting at home, as there was no edict against it, at least at that time as once was in another Kingdom, in Babylon. (27:6:6 ff). For without it, nothing may be received from God (58:11:6); but only through his autonomous mercy. Aren't you curious to know what happened in that meeting between a youth and the ruler of 127 countries, which act was unlawful under any circumstances, except, of course, the king spared the offender and allowed that his or her head still remain on his shoulders after being found guilty as charged? On that day, at that very moment, as this fasting youth approached, we heard that the king was sitting on his royal throne, facing the entrance into the palace. But why was he not elsewhere at this material time? Oh, let's read on, please. *When he saw Queen Esther standing there in the inner court, he welcomed her and held out the gold scepter to her.* So Esther approached and touched the end of the scepter.

No, the story did not end there, for the king immediately asked her, "What do you want, Queen Esther? What is your request? I will give it to you, even if what you want is half of the whole kingdom of 127 independent states." Do you know what Esther said? Oh no, fasting can make you bold and an award-winning actor. She just said, "Let the president and prime minister come *today* to the banquet I have prepared," and she said no more.

Mind you, the fast was still on, and it was the last day. It will be over by midnight that very day, which, if you were a part after the last prayer session, which may shoot past twelve or may be just before it, you will be ready to drink water and eat some fruits before the time for more solid meals. Immediately on hearing this invitation, the king turned to court officials standing by since, usually, the king sees no one alone in the palace. There have been disaster before elsewhere in this world because a monarch did just that—Ehud and Eglon (7:3:19). Then the king said, "Tell Haman to come *quickly* to a banquet as Esther has requested." Really thought he should say, "Tell him to come *quickly* to his death," but oh no, there is a time for everything (21:3:1). So it was, same day at the emergency banquet borne through fasting and prayer, as guests were all seated and eating and drinking with attendants all around, that the king wasted to time to repeat the question he asked while alone with the queen in the palace: "Now tell me what you really want. What is your request? I will give it to you even if it is half the kingdom!" But how did youth Esther respond? This is what she said: "This is my request and deepest wish. If I have found favor with the king, and if it pleases the king to grant my request and to do what I ask, please come with Haman tomorrow to the banquet that I will prepare for you. Then I will explain what this is all about." One thing I don't want you, my reader, to lose sight of is that this was not part of the deal between this youth and her guardian. He only solicited her assistance to make a case for the deliverance of the Jews before her husband so as not to be wiped out—nothing more and nothing less; but we observed that there was a fight, a battle of words, between these two a short while ago. And how it started and ended, we are all aware since it was in the open and through an intermediary. But where did this timid youth get such wisdom and courage? Just two words and we shall move on: *upbringing* and *fasting*. But there is a name I have not mentioned, should I? the Holy Spirit. But as Prime Minister Haman was exiting the banquet to his home, at the palace gate, he saw Mordecai, as usual not bowing unto him nor giving him due honor. So Prime Minister Haman was furious at the sight of gateman Mordecai for not standing up or trembling nervously before him when he was passing by as he had made all others to do in the name of the king. Yet he restrained himself and went home where he called his inner circle and gave them a mixed bundle of news of sadness and joy. Let us consider the joy aspect first: He talked about his immense wealth and also his number of children (when some don't even have any). He also bragged about the honors he had received. Remember, from nowhere, he was promoted above all the members of the supreme council to become prime minister, plus other accolades received from the supreme ruler, though not mentioned. Finally, the latest, he was invited to the banquet of the queen with the king, which he went to hurriedly giving him no time to brag about it before it was staged. He did not stop there. Let me give you this last bit as the prime minister actually stated it: "And that is not all! Queen Esther invited only me (underline mine) and the king himself to the banquet she prepared for us. And she has invited me to dine with her and the king again tomorrow." Next, this man then talked about his sadness, in his very words again, "But this is all worth nothing as long as I see Mordecai the Jew just sitting there at the gate!" Is he a normal human being, you will wonder, for in addition to all he listed above, he also wanted human worship, as if he were a god, and if you remember the exact sin of Lucifer, the devil, when in heaven and even here on earth, I am sure you remember the three temptations of Jesus after this very subject we are discussing now, fasting, when Satan told the Son of God, "Bow down and worship me and I will give you what you come for—to save mankind and not have to go through the route of the crucifixion on the cross." So this prime minister left the banquet joyful and elated, but on his way out, just still within the confines of the palace, his joy was deflated as of air in a balloon, for he saw the queen's cousin Mordecai who choose to obey the second commandment and bow only to God. By the way, Mordecai had other titles like doesn't-take-no-for-an-answer man, tries-again-when-he-fails man, doesn't-give-up man, and one who obeys like an innocent child when an idea of a workable solution is proposed, even by an opponent, in a dialogue.

So to please Haman, his inner circle of spouse and friends suggested a simple solution to brighten up the oriental despot. This was to kill his only barrier of being a human god. So that all will now bow before him when they see him – and this murder ahead of the time when Mordecai's entire race will be blotted out and that within twenty-four hours even before the second night of banquet he had bragged about! But who is this God that some fear, serve and worship, what can he do and is there anything he cannot do? Can anything be too late for God that he becomes so helpless like the mortal man he created in the first place to replace Arch Angel Lucifer and the wicked angels that joined him in heaven to rebel against Almighty God and to want to topple him from His throne?

Do we still remember when God told a man he needed a sacrifice as usual of blood but of a human blood and that of his only son? And the man decided to do this sacrifice and traveled with his son alone to the place God had shown him, but as Abraham, for so was the man called lifted up a knife in his hand to slaughter his only son, God said **Stop**....and provided on the spot from nowhere a lamb for sacrifice instead of his only son. We can go on endlessly like God inviting another man to a mountain to commune with him and kept him there for 40 days and 40 nights without a taste of food nor water to drink, yet this man a prophet of the very God came down from the mountain alive and still went forward to minister. The story did not end there for almost immediately not sure now if it was the same day or the day after, he was told to return for a second fasting of 40 days and 40 nights – which again he did successfully and also did not die nor faint - because God helped him!

Am sure you too, can testify to what this God can do, may be if not in your own life but in lives of some others you might have witnessed in your short span of life. May I continue with more accounts of what men and women have achieved through the help of God? May be not. Just one more case study? There was this young lady who with another got married to two immigrant brothers: sons of a widow which came with their parents some years back to this pagan nation because of lack of bread at home. Not too long after the two brothers died too – leaving the two daughters-in-law and the widow. Then the widow heard that back in her country things had turned around so decided to return. She however expected the daughters-in-law, to remain in their pagan country of birth concerning which God had said, even to four generations, no citizen of that nation plus another (Ammon) should enter the Temple of God for anything. Meaning at Believers' Temple too, until four generations had passed some people should not be allowed in! But do you know what happen to one of these two daughters-in-law? She became an ancestor of Jesus Christ – the Son of God, Ruth the Moabitess! Once after her sister-in-law returned and the mother-in-law was trying to convince her to return, turn back and not follow her back to the Promised Land, hear what she said: ***Don't ask me to leave you and turn back. Wherever you go, I will go; wherever you live, I will live. Your people will be my people, and your God will be my God. Wherever you die, I will die, and there will I be buried. May the Lord punish me severely if I allow anything but death to separate us! (8:1:16-17).*** Ruth was willing to learn from a godly elderly woman, a mother-in-law which she turned into a mother while reciprocally, she became more than 7 sons to her. What motivated her, what did she see? Faith of cause but do we see ***faith*** which elsewhere has been defined as ***the evidence of things not seen? (58:11:1)*** There is nothing this God cannot do for those that put their trust in Him and also obey Him.

CHAPTER 6

THE ROLE OF THE HOLY SPIRIT

Did I mention the Holy Spirit a short while ago? Divine intervention, what is it? This is a second question for your consideration; where will consider how soon, or how exactly God interferes in human affairs that beats the scheduling arrangements of the best planners. For starters let us consider the case of a man, Eliezer of Damascus, the eldest steward of another man Abraham, a millionaire that had only one son on a mission to find a wife for his son in another land. Things went so well without human intervention that the man bowed down and burst out in praise at last and said: ***Blessed be the LORD God of my master Abraham, who hath not left destitute my master of his mercy and truth: I being in the way, the LORD led me to the house of my master's brethren.*** (1:24:27).

What about during the inauguration of the very first Last Supper around the time of Jesus' Crucifixion when he sent two of his disciples to go and and sight the venue of that feast without given them any concrete address nor description, he merely said to Peter and John,....***Go and prepare us the passover, that we may eat. And they said unto him, Where will thou that we prepare? And he said unto them, Behold, when ye are entered into the city, <u>there shall a man met you, bearing a pitcher of water; follow him</u> into the house he entereth in. And ye shall say unto the good-man of the house, The master saith unto thee, Where is the guestchamber, where I shall eat the passover with my disciples? And he shall shew you a large upper room furnished: there make ready*** (41:22:8-12). But Jesus didn't tell them at what time they shall meet the man but controlled the independent movements of two different and independent parties. For all it is worth, the man carrying the pitcher of water might even not have known he was being followed! What if he

---

33

had decided to stop over somewhere to quickly do something? No it didn't happen that way to fault the prediction of Jesus. I want to give more examples. In the first example given above when a match maker adventured to look for a bride for a groom, even when everything seem okay, there was a fresh problem of delay and a complete breakdown of plans because the steward wanted to depart with the bride and some suggested that the bride stays at least 10 days more! So it was decided ...*We will call the damsel, and inquire at her mouth. And they called Rebekah, and said unto her, Wilt thou go with this man? And she said, I will go.* (1:24:57-58) What if she had refused to go? Oh no, not in God's scheme of things, everything always fit together perfectly.

Or should we consider the case of a holy man that was falsely accused unlawfully tried and locked up for years after dreams of greatness! According to the story, this believer momentarily shifted his trust away from God to a prisoner who had completed his prison sentence or was it a pardon he received and this holy man now said to the pardoned and discharged prisoner: *do make mention of me unto Pharaoh, and bring me out of this (prison) house:* He didn't stop there and when on to say *For indeed I was stolen away from out of the land of the Hebrews: and here also have I done nothing that they should put me in the dungeon.* (1:40:15) That chapter of this story didn't end with the plea and or complaint, but with the following words: *Yet did not the chief butler remember Joseph, but forgat him* (1:40:23) But how did the story really end, God that is never too late nor too early after two full years that a man made an appeal to another man, God himself started the mechanism when he gave dreams to the Supreme Ruler but at the same time blocked all his salaried seers from the ability to interpret his dreams, making the pardoned prisoner to repent when he said to the confused dreamer: *I do remember my fault today....in jail...there was a young man, an Hebrew...he interpreted to us our dreams....* We cannot go into the detail of that story but hear what the confused dreamer King said to the imprisoned holy man Joseph as conclusion: *Forasmuch as God hath shewed thee all this, there is none so discreet and wise as thou art: Thou shalt be over my house, and according unto thy word shall all my people be ruled:*

only in the throne will be greater than thou art (he went on to say
to say to holy Joseph) *See, I have set thee over all the land of Egypt..*
(1:41:39-41). Do we therefore see how God maintain precision in
all he does never too late or too early?

Let us continue about God and his plans, how he fulfills his plan
and will: a old man was told to come to a holy gathering with all
his sons, yet even though he had 8 sons, decided not to hear the
prophet's instruction but translated it himself to fulfill his his
own agenda. And that meeting was the coronation of the second
king of Israel after the institution of the monarchy. The old man
got the prophet of God fooled who was determined to choose
one of the brothers which this man paraded as all his sons. The
prophet at last became confused because he did not receive the
confirmation of God in all his preliminary choices, so he asked:
Are here all thy (male) children? Not until then did the old man
said: *There remaineth yet the youngest, and, behold, he keepeth the
sheep* prompting the the prophet to say, *send and fetch him: for
we will not sit down till he come hither.* And so a candidate whose
name was not on the original the ballot became the inaugurated
successor—which again show us how God moves! What shall we
say more? That God willing to get his Son into the world to show
lost mankind the way back to God had to allow what have never
been done—that a virgin should conceive and give birth to a Son
of Man and/or the Son of God! Let us again consider another
example, the parting of the Red Sea—while a nation passed as if
on dry ground, the army of another nation assaying to cross the
same Red sea as if a dry land but all perished in the sea because
the God that made the sea dry land for Israel to pass through,
later drawned the entire army of Egypt—same day! I want to
go on: For forty years a migrant nation of close to a million was
sustained by food and water without anyone sowing or repeating
with water sometimes obtained from dry hard rocks! What about
the provision of food for this men women and children, which
in the night was nonexistent or absent but in morning light food
literally from heaven now covered the face of the earth—every
day for 40 years!

So in the story we are considering, not surprisingly, that night God as usual demonstrated his power.

For that night, we are told the king had trouble sleeping, and instead of reaching out to the only thing or one he needed to make him complete, he reached out to another thing—thing, I say, not people, since there are people at his beck and call, not for help to go back to bed, but he ordered an attendant (person) to bring a book (thing), the book of the history of his reign so it could be read unto him. As the book was being read to him, the king commanded the reader to stop in no other portion but at a portion on the mention of the name of a man whom the king had very recently signed a decree that in a year's time, his entire race should be wiped off the surface of the earth. At the mention of the name and act of this man, the king ordered, "Stop there!" The king just discovered, he heard read, an account of the man Mordecai. Remember him? He was the one who would not bow to man but to God alone and who had exposed the plot of two security/ military officers, Bigthana and Teresh, who guarded the door to the king's private quarters. They had planned to assassinate King Xerxes for removing a reigning queen, who most probably staged a comeback but failed again. Remember when all the virgins gathered again after the installation of Queen Esther (17:2:19) to repeat the contest and maybe give the king the people's choice and not the choice of God (America in this year: Hillary Clinton versus Ben Carlson or as it now appear Donald Trump)?

So the king asked, "What reward or recognition did we ever give Mordecai for this?" And the answer came: Nothing has been done for him. Is that really so? Do you not expect to be honored for everything you do, especially with distinction, when no other person reached the same mark, in your office or even in life and you then want to do something about your not being recognized? Of course, you are right since God might have forgotten or fallen asleep—is that so? But wait a minute, what does the word of God say here? Read with me: *The one who watches over you will not slumber. Indeed, he who watches over Israel never slumbers nor sleeps* (19:121:2-4).

Just then, at that very moment, it was the first watch of the morning light now. The reading of the records must have taken so many hours, in which the seeker of sleep did not get what he wanted but instead had been listening to a news broadcast being read to him, taking them all in and not dozing off to sleep until the command "Stop there!" rang out when the bit of the assassination plot was mentioned and when the name of the savior—the savior of the king's life—was also mentioned. And when the early morning visitor was ushered in, it was for the sole purpose of getting a decree signed for the execution of a man who just completed a three-day fast of no food and no water at the order of a youth, a female. Needless to say Haman never had the opportunity to make that request unto the man that had never denied him anything he ever asked for, including that fellow men bow to him as god when and wherever they see him. On admittance, he was welcomed by the king with a question: "What should I do to honor a man who truly pleases me?"

Can things suddenly change and turn around for good for a man or a woman who is on death row and destined to die within 24 hours? Whatever answer anyone may come forward with, that is exactly how the fate of Mordecai the Jew turned around completely! Probably those that built the gallows and they who had be earmarked to execute this prayer and fasting Mordecai had been paid and are waiting at the execution site in Haman's home while dispatchers had been sent to Mordecai's home and/or later to the King's gate where he can be easily found, to take him and bring him to the execution site. But the story did not end or go that way. Instead the question asked and answered as we shall see in the next paragraph was what to do to honor Mordecai, and certainly not what to do to kill him!

How would you have answered were the question addressed to you? Though no other reader will hear what you say now, but do venture an answer and probably write it down before reading on for maximum reade benefit. And to his credit, he thought for a second, the sure way to give an answer, to first think and not just open ones mouth and blot out the first idea that proceeds from within. We need to think when we are at a crossroad of decision. Remember youth Esther, when she gave all reasonable answers to her mentor seeking a small favor from her, which she did not consider small but extremely dangerous, arguing that it is not possible, that such request shouldn't be made to anyone, especially to one's beloved daughter, a youth, what response did she give? The best quoted verse in all of Holy Scripture already quoted above, "Go gather all the Jews . . . and fast ye for me, and neither eat nor drink, three days, night or day: I also and my maidens will fast likewise . . ."

What did the prime minister say? How did he reason in arriving at his answer to the king concerning the man he came to seek permission to murder, although unknown to him at the time? He reasoned, "Who will the king wish to honor more than me?" *No other,* he might have concluded, so he replied, after careful thinking, which really is required for those that shun and reject indifference and minimize emotions, which is apathy, whether youth or the elderly, saying, "If the king wishes to honor someone, he should bring out one of the (i) king's own royal robes, (ii) as well as a horse that the king himself has ridden, one with (iii) a royal emblem on its head, and (iv) let the robes and the horse be handed over to one of the king's most noble officials, (v) who would see to it that the man whom the king wishes to honor is dressed in the king's robes and (vi) led through the city square on the king's horse while (vii) the official, as they go, shouts, "This is what the king does for someone he wishes to honor!" How do you think the king answered his prime minister? Excellent! He said and went on to say, "Take the robes and the horse, and do just as you have said for Mordecai the Jew, who sits at the gate of the palace (and) leave out nothing that you have suggested." So Haman carried out royal instruction as he had suggested to the king and which the king had endorsed hook, line, and sinker. Remember the king's edict that all should bow before Haman when he is spotted anywhere? So he took the robes and the crown and put them on Mordecai, and let him ride on the king's own horse, and led him through the city square, shouting, "This is what the king does for someone he wishes to honor." Do you know what happened afterward? Simple,

Mordecai returned to his duty post—the palace gate. Oh my, it was a gateman that a Prime Minister had to bow before, going on foot and singing his praise at the top of his voice so that all could hear, including those asleep, to suddenly jump out of sleep and see the Prime Minister bowing and worshiping the porter-gateman as the latter rides on the king's own horse. You enemies will bow for you if you fast and pray, and never despondent whatever attack comes your way.

But as for Haman, he hurried dejected and completely humiliated. And as usual, at home, where his inner circle of friends had been waiting since early morning to see, read, and handle the king's edict to terminate the life of Mordecai the Jew. Instead, Haman's inner circle heard the story of shame, defeat, and disgrace he narrated to them step-by step of all that happened to him from inside the palace to the city gate, Mordecai's duty post, and to the city square. Granted these couldn't have heard about the unfolding of the drama that started in the palace when the king sought counsel about how to honor someone and then asking Mr. Prime Minister, what should we do? But did they not hear or see what happened in town between Mordecai and his archenemy Haman? I mean, all of or at least some of the ten sons of Haman who usually should be bragging about it downtown on what they have learned from their father to now see him bowing before a commoner gateman. It must have been a very sad gathering, yet they had to hurry to discuss and conclude against the coming of the palace carriers that would convey the prime minister to the second night of the banquet. And after all was said and done, the committee came up with a resolution and said, "Since Mordecai—this man that humiliated you—is of Jewish birth, you will never succeed in your plans against him. It will be fatal to continue opposing him." Little did these know that their utterance formed a prediction against the edict of complete annihilation of the Jews the following year. They could not have even imagined that the prime minister might not, would not, return home to his beloved wife, But he did return but only to die by execution and not to children, to eat, play, or to sleep. Yes he did return to die unfortunately. But the conference was cut short for while they were still talking, the king's special officers arrived and quickly conveyed the disgraced Prime Minister Haman to the second day of the banquet of wine that Esther the queen had prepared.

Given the report Ham brought home to his wife and friends when he got back from honoring Mordecai and singing his praises all around the city, and the sudden and immediate transportation of Haman to the the second day of the banquet of wine, can somebody just imagine how the conversation between his wife and friends continued thereafter? No matter what they thought, am sure it would never have crossed the mind of any of them, that on that very day, the pole prepared by Haman for Mordecai will actually be used to hang Haman on that fateful day! For he did returned home after the abrupt end of the party on that second and final day of the feast, but not voluntarily but in chains and straight to his death at very gallows prepared to a man who could pray. What about you, can you pray?

CHAPTER 7

IT IS BANQUET TIME: ARE YOU READY?

Can anyone tell us how this banquet of wine would look for these three—a lady and two imminent gentlemen? I mean, their individual states of mind as they come together to a feast. The state of mind of Haman is the easiest to guess, given all that transpired for him earlier on that day. Whereas the king shared part of the Haman's experience that day since it was him who commanded Haman to bow in public before a man he described as his honorary, the very man unknown to the king he had granted Haman's wish not only to kill him but all of his race, including his own wife and queen, whose origin nobody actually yet knew as at that time, since it was still a secret, and the mass murder to be effected within one year. Haman, no doubt, was still basking in the false glory of being the only one in the entire land the queen had invited, alongside the king, to attend this dinner. Maybe had he known at the onset that it was going to be a two-day dinner, he could at least have been proud being the special guest with the king on the very first night to whoever gets the invitation for the second and final night, which would be his rival and enemy, going from what we have known about this man so far. But as the story goes, nobody, not even the king, knew that the banquet will run for more than a night, save Esther, the queen; and we guess her guardian-father, who was recently honored by the king, did not know too. He had commanded youth Esther to go talk to her husband and didn't care how she achieved this assignment, so Esther too would not have had any reason to inform him how she would go about fulfilling this task nor the exact time she will get it done. All they had in common was to pray and to fast for three days and nights, not eating food nor drinking even water as it were being left on her own, one might say, but oh no, not alone, for she still had the Holy Spirit, a divine part of the Trinity, who could operate without being seen but often is seen and could take any form like fire, wind, voice, or even a four-footed animal to guide her, just to give four examples of the ways he has manifested himself of God.

Another person coming to the party whose frame of mind we are to watch was the king himself. He was so curious wanting to know what the queen really wanted to warrant her staging a party and even inviting the second in command. No wonder he made extraordinary promises and assurances before actually hearing the queen's request: *even half the kingdom*. This at least should have been an eye-opener to the prime minister that despite his high office, he really meant nothing to the king, else should he not have promised just a third of the kingdom, with a possible third in the event, going to Prime Minister Haman who the king must have known is fond of making requests and/or demands, who even promised to give money to the government should his latest request, now granted though, be seemingly uneasy to fulfill or damn impossible. Finally, we should consider the state of mind of the queen coming to this party: peaceful, fully in control, and confident while getting ready to strike at the most appropriate moment. I guess she could have still had a day extension to her banquet had she not received a green light from her main partner at this time: the Holy Ghost.

Though not mentioned here elsewhere, the word said, "As many as are led by the Holy Ghost, they are the sons (I guess and daughters) of God" (45:8:14). And so to this banquet, all three arrived on the second night of the feast, and as usual, without much ado, the banquet commenced.

Though not mentioned elsewhere, the word said, "As many as are led by the Holy Ghost, they are the sons of God" (45:8:14) (I guess and daughters too though as . . . there is neither male nor female in Christ (48:3:38).

And without much ado, Esther began, "If I have found favor in thy sight, O King, and if it pleases the king, let my life be given me at my petition and my people at my request."

This wasn't her whole request to the king, her husband, but it behooves us to stop here and to ponder. Esther must have believed Mordecai's utterance during their battle of words to go or not to go to the king, when he said to her, "If you don't go, help will come from another source for the Jews, but you will perish in the palace (Esther:4:14, my paraphrase).

But the queen was in the palace where, literally, she just could not be reached by the edict to kill all Jews, even if it were known that she was a Jew, yet she said in the opening of her petition, "Let my life be given me at my petition," and that is faith to completely believe the word of God through his prophet of the hour. Or did Moses act differently when he identified with the suffering Jews in Egypt though raised in the palace (Heb 11:24–25)? So whatever the believer's current position in life, this matters little, vis-a-vis what we can achieve or do moving in divine flow. "For we are sold," Esther continued, "I and my people, to be *destroyed*, to be *slain*, and to *perish*. But if we had been sold for bondmen and bond women, I had held my tongue, although the enemy could not countervail the king's damage. Let us just put ourselves in that banquet as we observe the dialogue between the queen and king in the presence of Prime Minister Haman immediately following:

King: Who is he, and where is he that durst presume in his heart to do so?

Queen: The adversary and enemy is this wicked Haman.

Then, we were told, Haman was afraid before the king and queen. Next, the king got up to move away and adjust himself to the news he just heard—someone planning to kill his wife, an information he has been bargaining to be told with very high rewards. But on returning to the banquet, what did he witness? He found Haman on the same sofa on which the queen was reclining. True, he had originally got up from his seat and stood on his feet to, as was recorded, make a request for his life to Esther, the queen, but how come, on the king's reappearance, he found Haman by his queen, lying beside her? Can somebody imagine that scenario, how the king felt on his return to the banquet of wine? He was stunned, and all he muttered out was just a question and not a command: "Will he force the queen also before me in the house?" And instantaneously, the face of Prime Minister Haman was covered in preparation for execution. Quickly, another official announced a stake for execution already prepared that same day for the execution of the saver of the king's life, the man the king delighted to honor, by the prime minister, to which the king just said, "Hang him thereon," and was then satisfied. But what really can believers not do or achieve in this life, and no matter how enormous, colossal or mighty any problem facing the believer may be, should these have any cause to fear? The answer is a simple **No** or **Never**—your choice. Is victory not predetermined for those who love God and are God according to his purpose? If these things are true how then should men of different ages and races live their lives in the temporary abode called earth? Yet some will still mortgage their souls for temporal gains in this world and so forfeit an eternal resting place in heaven to roast in burning hell! But we shall overcome some day.

CHAPTER 8

SECRETS AND THE DIVULGING OF THEM RE. OLOFOFO

Secrets—why keep them or who keeps them? And is there any disadvantage in not keeping them? How long should secrets be kept, if at all, forever? Those that expose secrets, what are they called? And is there any inherently good or bad about such people? *Olofofo* (Yoruba), that is what **MD** calls them, simply means the revealer of secrets, which they are not supposed to, I guess. But when **MD** says this, she means it in a negative way, a derogation. But another person considers this attribute differently; in fact, the person says the revealer of secrets is a name and/or attribute of God (27 2:22). But elsewhere, we were told in Deuteronomy 29:29, the secret things belong unto the Lord our God, but those things which are revealed belong unto us and to our children forever that we may do all the words of this law (Bible). So who should keep secrets, and why should these be kept, and are there times when this should be made known?

As I consider this matter, two names come to mind: One is *Bola Tinubu*, a one-time governor of Lagos State in Nigeria, who, I hear, have ties in Chicago and who may have attended University of Chicago, where he was said to have graduated with a bachelor's degree in 1979 from Chicago State University. The other was simply called *Mordecai*, born in Israel and, like Bola Tinubu, lived for a long time in a foreign land, a great father who brought up an outstanding youth. As for Bola Tinubu, a two-term governor, I am not sure if he kept secrets or didn't care to keep secrets, but I accidentally heard, in the third week of December 2015, secrets about him that astounded me, for example that his personal wealth surpassed that of seven states in Nigeria, having a total of thirty-six states. Was this a rumor or fact, and if fact, did Tinubu care that it was revealed, or is he covering this up in some diabolical ways via others that front for him as my source stated? Leaving Tinubu now, I turn to another man that actually kept at least a secret, Mordecai, for he told the queen to conceal her origin for as long and nobody knew, until he blew it out by the message he sent to her through an intermediary that she had to go plead for her people. As a beauty contestant, Esther had not told anyone of her nationality and family background because Mordecai had directed her not to do so, we read in (17:2:10); and elsewhere, shortly after Esther's coronation as queen, when there was another contest staged, which invariably was of no consequence as Esther remained the queen, it was also said in (17:2:20) that Esther continued to keep her family background and nationality a secret, and she was still following Mordecai's directions, just as she did when she lived in his home, though now the queen of the empire.

On the day Prime Minister Haman was executed did King Xerxes give the estate of Haman, the Jews' enemy, to Esther, the queen, we were told. The story went on, and Mordecai came before the king, for Esther had told what he was to her. The secret has now been revealed unto all. The new changes did not end there: There was a transfer of the office of the prime minister to Mordecai since Haman is now dead and of his estate also to Mordecai, the first by the king and the latter by the queen. One wonders if the covered facts, the secret, had not been revealed, what would have happened, for example what the king would have thought having passed on the estate of Haman to his queen for her to now passed it almost immediately to another man, a man she, on numerous, occasions had been observed sneaking out of the palace to see, though always briefly and in the open? So therefore, there is a time for everything, a time to keep silence and a time to speak (21:3:7). It, therefore, appears that no matter what is heavy on our mind to spill, there would always be an appropriate time to do so. But does revealing a carefully guarded secret solve every problem? I don't think so, at least not in the case of the impending annihilation of every Jew from the surface of the earth. It is true that Haman is now dead, but what about the king's decree that is still in effect? No wonder then Esther went again before the king, falling down at his feet and begging him with tears to stop the evil plot devised by Haman, the Agagite, against the Jews. And on being recognized, Esther wasted no time to deliver the message she was sent to deliver, which she initially refused because she thought this was an impossible mission before being suddenly reminded by the Holy Spirit of the method that cannot ever fail.

So Esther said, "(i) If it pleases the king, and (ii) if I have found favor with him, and (iii) if he think it is right, and (iv) if I am pleasing to him, then let there be a decree that reverses the orders of Haman, the son of Hammedatha the Agagite, who ordered that the Jews throughout all the king's provinces should be destroyed. For how can I endure to see my people and my family slaughtered and destroyed?"

In response to this additional plea from the queen, the king, knowing the enormous danger to the Jews of his decree in force, gave a forthright solution when he said, "Now go ahead and send a message to the Jews in the king's name, telling them *whatever* you want, and seal it with the king's signet ring." But remember that whatever has already been written in the king's name and sealed with his signet ring can never be revoked. And according to the records, on June 25, the king's secretaries were summoned, and a decree was written exactly as how Mordecai dictated, which was sent to the Jews, the highest officers, the governors, and the nobles of all the 127 provinces, stretching from India to Ethiopia. Further, the record shows the decree was written in the scripts and languages of all the people of the empire, including that of the Jews, in the name of the king, Xerxes, and sealed with the king's signet ring and that Mordecai sent the dispatches by swift messengers, who rode fast horses especially bred for the king's services (17:8–10).

Do we still remember how these all started? It all started after two very significant actions of a president: first, the coronation of a new queen from a slave race kept a top secret and an almost immediate appointment into a position that did not exist prior—yet higher than that of the Supreme Council of 7, that of a Prime Minister of a previously unknown man but from among the majority race— man that made himself a god and demanded worship by decree of the king and when just a single fellow, refused to worship or bow for a fellow human being, solely on religious grounds, the self proclaimed god, in chapter 3 verse 6 considered it scorn to lay hands on Mordecai alone; for the people of Mordecai has been made known to him: wherefore Haman sought to destroy all the Jews that were throughout the whole kingdom of king Xerxes, even the people of Mordecai. And although a date was carefully determined in the following year on March 7, Haman couldn't wait until the next year to exterminate this man and decided to kill him immediately for no additional offense, built the gallows and went to the king to get approval for the death sentence. Needless to say upon that very gallows did he die and the total destruction of the Jews the following year was still pending at the very moment in the rescue mission of a mere youth. So we now have two decrees of the king and president on ground the effective date of which was March 7 the following year. Unlike the first that permitted the Jews to be slaughtered, the king's latter decree gave the Jews in every city authority to unite to defend their lives. They were allowed to kill, to slaughter, and to annihilate anyone of any nationality or province who might attack them or their children and wives and to take the properties of their enemies.

A copy of this decree was issued as law in every province and proclaimed to all peoples so that the Jews would be ready to take revenge on their enemies on the appointed day. So urged by the king's command, the messengers rode out swiftly on fast horses bred for the king's service. The same decree was also proclaimed in the capital city of Susa. In spite of the sinister plot to kill a palace gateman and all his kin and kindred in a foreign land, who for no additional offense his day of death was fast forwarded by one year. But suddenly as a result of a simple command made by a youth to corporately pray and to fast for just 3 days and night without food or water, which order he faithfully carried out to the letter, the gateman walked out of the king's presence wearing a royal robe of blue and white; a great crown of gold; and an outer cloak of fine linen and purple, with everybody in the capital celebrating him! And all over this vast empire, believers were filled with joy and gladness and were honored everywhere. It was a common knowledge that everywhere the king's latest decree arrived, believers rejoiced, had a great celebration during this declared public festival and holiday. Additionally, so many citizens became believers for that became fashionable, when a short while earlier, it was either hatred or pity that was felt, for these were all that were condemned to die on the seventh of March the following year. All changed because of a youth, who was not apathetic, dared to face the problem ahead of her and did not resign to fate by saying or admitting what will be will be. You too can, as God never change and Jesus Christ is the same yesterday today and forever.

CHAPTER 9

THE ENCOUNTER

Can you, for a moment, envision the outcome of an encounter, which, by all intents and purposes, had been deemed fatal in your disfavor and now suddenly turned around against your attackers? And so on March 7 of the following year, two conflicting decrees of the king concerning one particular group of people were to be put into effect. On that day, the enemies of the Jews had hoped to overpower them, but quite the opposite happened. It was the Jews who overpowered their enemies. On this appointed day, the Jews had gathered in their cities throughout the king's provinces to attack anyone who tried to harm them. But no one could make a stand against them for everyone was afraid of them, we were told. Is this what believing prayer could do, especially when mingled with fasting? As the story went, all the nobles, the highest officers, the governors, and the royal officials of the provinces helped the Jews for fear of a former gateman who refused to bow nor worship a human being other than God Almighty. For this believing gateman has been promoted in this king's palace, and his fame spread everywhere throughout all the provinces as he became more and more powerful.

The turnaround events described in the above paragraph, which we shall return to in this chapter—what is it really called and what can we liken it to? It is a *movement*, the act or process of moving people or things from one place or position to another; also a tactical or strategic shifting of a military unit.

It could be defined as a progressive development of ideas towards a particular conclusion or a diffusely organized or heterogeneous group of people or organizations tending toward or favoring a generalized common goal. The above definition we obtain in part from Merriam-Webster Dictionaries. And can we see how things could turn? The annihilation of the Jews was already a forgone conclusion, they were already as good as dead, yes all of them. And such powers could be obtained from various sources including Nouveau Tech, mermaid spirit and such like sources which though could lead to impressive crowd effect maneuvering are negative and eventually results in apathy among whichever segment of society it was aimed at, not just the youth. We should remember that the Jews were done and or finished; the day of their massacre has been predetermined and suddenly things changed by turning exactly 180 degrees around because people prayed and fasted! For the Jews now had power over those that hated them—this through an assisting wind that overcame the contrary wind that began from the time when Heman was hung on the pole he prepared for Mordecai in his house ahead of the time when all Jews were to be slaughtered. Yes individuals are free to obtain powers from whatsoever source they choose and as numerous as these sources appear, they are all just two: good and evil.

On that appointed day, the Jews, with sword in hand, struck down their enemies—killing and annihilating them, and satisfying their vengeance on their enemies. In the capital alone, five hundred people were killed by the Jews, plus the ten sons of the deceased prime minister, who were his pride: (1) Parshandatha, (2) Dalphone, (3) Aspatha, (4) Poratha, (5) Adalia, (6) Aridatha, (7) Parmashta, (8) Arisa, (9) Aridai, and (10) Vaizatha.

And in all their killing, they did not, as the decree permitted, take any plunder. And not only in the capital city did the Jews record victories over their enemies but also throughout the 127 provinces of the empire, where in all seventy-five thousand people slaughtered, not of innocent civilians but of those that hated them and wanted to exterminate them completely. As all this killing was going on, hear what the king was recorded to have said to that fasting youth who doubled as the queen of the land after he learned that five hundred people had been killed by the Jews in his capital: "But now, what more do you want? It will be granted to you; tell me and I will do it" (17:912). So the queen replied that the slaughter in the capital city be repeated the next day as well as hang up in display for all to see the ten sons of that wicked tyrant who, because one man offended him, was not content to deal with him as he saw fit but decided to erase his entire race from the surface of the earth. This request, the king granted as three hundred more were killed in the capital while the rest of the empire had a holiday that day, celebrating their victories. Those in the capital then celebrated their victory on March 9, making March 8 and 9 days of Purim celebrations of the Jews, a name borrowed from the process the deposed and executed erstwhile Prime Minister Haman used for determining the March 7 execution date for all the Jews but which eventually became a day of victory for them instead.

And so just merely because of two simple acts by two youths, for indeed Mordecai too was a youth, a mere cousin to Esther who had the responsibility of fatherhood thrust on him because of the premature death of his uncle and aunt, of *refusal to worship idol* and the *exercise of the biblical injunction of fasting*, a whole race in a foreign land could now make laws and establish decrees by letter which was confirmed by Esther and written down by Mordecai in the records of a foreign nation.

CHAPTER 10

CONCLUSION

We all have different roles to play in life, and these roles are unique to individuals, no matter where they are stationed around the globe, whether male or female, as a teenager, a youth in the prime of life, or a senior citizen. The Creator expects us to make the best of our situation, and he has left us more than enough resources to go through life. In fact, our abilities are limitless. Or who would expect an orphan child raised by a relatively unknown guardian to become the next queen of a vast empire, with this unknown guardian now known everywhere and respected by his people, even becoming a prime minister in a foreign land? Yes, everyone's situation is unique, but no matter how hopeless things may seem along the way, it can be turned around by the simple act of obedience to elders and/or parents, in addition to a belief in a sovereign being, the Creator, who will request at the end of time for all living to give an account of how the individual's time on earth was spent.

What will be said about you after you were gone? We shall now close with two men: Xerxes and Mordecai even though this book is about a female youth or youths in general and not about male adults, since our lives here on earth are intertwine together according to Sociologist John Donn, Xerxes went on to do great especially through what the imposition of taxes could do even unto distant lands through the assistance of a believing wife by his side. And this is surprising especially since beautiful women have been known to be wanton, self indulgent and almost always godless and can anyone remember Jezebel? This king, we were told, was really great. And as for Prime Minister Mordecai, whom the king had promoted with authorities next to himself, he was very great among his people, we were also told, for he was held in high esteem because he continued to work for the good of his people and to speak up for the welfare of all their descendants. Our narration is over, but just a question if I may, was it right for Mordecai to adamantly refuse to bow to Prime Minister-god Haman when it was the politically correct thing to do since everyone else was doing it? Should he have risked his life and everyone else's life like that? What if God did not come to his rescue? What if the new status of that orphan-youth-turned-queen had gotten into her head and she damned the consequences to risk her life by going to the king, which was not according to law, but she just refused to obey the instruction of her guardian-father since she is now above all in the land? The what-ifs are indeed interesting and sweet to consider, but could God have failed to have her back as we say? No, never, he neither slumber nor sleep, and he is always on time. Remember, Mordecai even told his ward, the queen, during the hot exchanges between them both that if she refused to go and speak for the believers, help will arise from another source and she in the palace with all hers will perish (17:4:13–14). But who is to be blamed here—is it Mordecai that we say took a risk not to bow to any man and damned the consequence or the ex-prime minister-god Haman, a peacock that wanted human worship at all cost? Who did he think he was? Somebody elsewhere was greeted on his arrival with worship and falling down/bowing down when he arrived at a function where he was speaker and guest of honor not just by anybody else but by an army general, who promptly told the greeter, "Don't do it. I am a man like you" (44:25–26). Yet Haman decided to not just kill a man but his entire race because one man decided not to bow to a fellow man but to the Almighty God alone. Haman probably thought the disobedience would be multiplied by some others in the empire. But was Mordecai really justified in not following the conventional wisdom? Just one more example of politically incorrect actions one might say before we conclude: *And I fell at his feet to worship him. And he said to me, See that do it not: I am thy fellow servant, and of thy brethren that have the testimony of Jesus: worship God: for the testimony of Jesus is the spirit of prophecy.* It was not enough for Haman to be executed once; he should have been executed multiple times, assuming it was possible to bring him back to life each time he died for the act of execution to be repeated on him before eventually going to burn in hell for compelling humans to break the two foremost commandments: the first two of ten, in not giving allegiance to another God than the God of Israel and not bow to anyone or anything, including the almighty dollar. But this epilogue isn't about Haman but about two men: Xerxes and Haman. But in closing, I wish it be about two blood relations: Haman, the prime minister, and not with Xerxes, the king, for they have no blood tie, but with Esther, the queen. So somebody tell me who did better: teenager Esther or young adult Mordecai? Whichever answer you give will be okay because they both participated in the three-day Estheric fast and both reaped immensely therefrom. It is time for you to shine as they both did young wo(man). The world we live should not rot but glow, and who else is best to run the affairs of our world as presidents and governors? Those who bow to money and want worship or those who bow to the Creator God alone, can communicate effectively with him, and are ready to serve their fellow men and women to bring about a better world order, especially in these end time? But there is an urgent need for man to believe in God this his son Jesus Christ that historically walked this earth years after the events that this book in the main dealt with. So many things transpired but all that could be said is **...but God**! Or how do we explain the fact that one man came to the king to sign the death warrant of another man and end up same day bowing down before the one on death row and showering him praises all through the city square and sweating profusely in the process and eventually ending up being put to death on the very gallows he prepared for that his enemy?

What about a king that did not know what petitioner desired and swore that he would grant whatever the request may be to the tune of half of his kingdom! Or the same king who could not sleep one night and instead of taking sleeping pills or subjecting himself to whatever the physician prescribed for his relief instead called for a book to be read before him, a book of remembrance and heard about a good man that did a good deed but was neither remembered nor rewarded and he fixed the problem right there and then. This is more miraculous because the good man got recognition and reward on the very date of his execution according to the deposed and late Prime Minister's time table! And in all these events and occurrences the part played by youths cannot be overemphasized. In this last chapter we have attempted to consider who the hero (or heroin) of the book is, but without God who answers prayer can there be a human hero, who actually said: *without me, you can do nothing* (42:15:5). In this mind set therefore, let us consider one, two or three more cases where God had caused it to happen for mortal man and that in a very big way, the last case not being a mortal man like the first two but relating to God's very Son who was conceived of virgin Mary.

Usually in our world, we see the cases of the oppressed and their oppressors: the Syrian had raided Israel and had taken many captive including one little girl about the age of our heroine Esther or may be a little younger who now served as maid at the the home of the army General who captured her in war. On seeing the army General, the husband of her mistress completely infested with leprosy she passed a side comment to her mistress when she said*"Would God my lord were with the prophet in Samaria! For he would recover him of his leprosy"* This side comment was relayed to the Syrian king who then sent to his Israeli counterpart just defeated in war that: *Now when this letter is come unto thee, behold, I have therewith sent Naaman my servant to thee, that thou mayest recover him of his leprosy.*(12:5:6). This letter came as an utter shock to the Israeli monarch who tore his royal robes immediately. And when the prophet had this he took charge and ordered the sick of leprosy to *Go and wash in Jordan seven times, and thy flesh shall come again to thee, and thou shalt be clean* which happened exactly as the man of God predicted for his flesh came again like unto the flesh of a little child, and he was clean—another example of what God can do through man.

What about another oppressive case of master servant relationship also between two king: a rejected king and an incoming king. The rejected king persecuted the incoming king even to strange cities to snatch off his life. We will just give one example of what God could do and actually did. To hunt down one man, the rejected king came out with 3,000 chosen men on the hint that David was at hill Harchilah in Jeshinon which rumor was confirmed to be true. What happened next was very surprising. David with just a man came to the camp of 3000 + 1 men at night and found them all sleeping. *So David took the spear and the cruse of water from Saul's bolster; and they gat them away, and no man saw it, nor knew it, neither awaked: for they were all asleep; <u>because a deep sleep from the LORD was fallen upon them</u>* (9:26:12).

The oppressor still seek to hunt the oppressed even in today's America and there seems to be no justice. Or how can a city mail traffic violation tickets to an address it knows the motorist have moved away from and having the motorist's new address on its record which the motorist notified the city of with the payment of a fee? And then boot a car purchased by loan with a Mercedes Benz trade-in and the car now disappeared between the city of Chicago and Ally bank, the bank that financed the new car purchase and when the motorist sued for redress the Supreme Court of the United State failed to give justice to the aggrieved motorist but instead threw out the case instructing that the Clerk of the Court should never filed non criminal cases instituted by this particular motorist petitioner, who now speedily paid the required fee via a miraculous provision in a timely manner, yet the case was again thrown out with the enclosed certified check with not fresh explanation? *See Plates/Exhibits immediately following the last example.*

What about Jesus the God-man that was nailed alive to the Cross in Calvary, suffered bled and died. Water even gushed from his side and was buried in a secured tomb. Yet the great stone at the gate of the tomb was rolled away that women who came early on Sunday morning to anoint a dead body could enter without assistance and become the first witnesses to carry the news after being told by an Angel: *Fear not ye: for I know that ye seek Jesus, which was crucified. He is not here: for he is risen, as he said. Come, see the place where the Lord lay. And go quickly, and tell his disciples that he is risen from the dead; and, behold he goeth before you into Galilee; there shall ye see him: lo, I have told you.* (40:28:4-7)

The God of the youth that dared to believe, to pray and to fast can grant you victory too as he has done to so many since the world began that apathy whatever the cause whether you are an adult or a youth will not be your experience. Regarding the apparent failed legal system in Chicago 1 and Chicago 2 of Cook County, Illinois Supreme Court in Springfield and Supreme Court of the United States in Washington DC that has been referenced in this work, it should be remembered that the God that delivered Confessors Shadrach Meshach and Abednego from a fiery furnace of fire because of their stand of faith allowed Deacon Stephen, the first Christian martyr to be stoned to death also for his faith! ...*all these worketh that one and the selfsame Spirit, dividing to every man severally as He will* (46:12:11)

Supreme Court of the United States
Office of the Clerk
Washington, DC 20543-0001

Scott S. Harris
Clerk of the Court
(202) 479-3011

April 4, 2016

Mr. Gregg Moore
3057 West Argyle Street
Chicago, IL 60625

Re: Gregg Moore
v. City of Chicago, Illinois
No. 15-7964

Dear Mr. Moore:

The Court today entered the following order in the above-entitled case:

The motion of petitioner for leave to proceed *in forma pauperis* is denied, and the petition for a writ of certiorari is dismissed. See Rule 39.8. As the petitioner has repeatedly abused this Court's process, the Clerk is directed not to accept any further petitions in noncriminal matters from petitioner unless the docketing fee required by Rule 38(a) is paid and the petition is submitted in compliance with Rule 33.1. See *Martin* v. *District of Columbia Court of Appeals*, 506 U. S. 1 (1992) *(per curiam)*.

Sincerely,

Scott S. Harris, Clerk

SUPREME COURT
OF THE UNITED STATES

Case Nos.: 15-7964,.....

Moore v. City of Chicago	– CIVIL
Moore v. 3 Objectors: Robert I Sherman.. + Illinois Board of Election & Bruce Rauner	– POLITICAL
Moore v. People of the State of Illinois	– CRIMINAL

To the entire U S Supreme Court Judges + Clerk of the Court

Earlier this month an order of April 4, 2016 and mailed on April 5, 2016 was received by indigent Pro Se. Petitioner Gregg Moore and signed by Scott S. Harris, Clerk of the court of the denial of petitioner's motion for leave to proceed in *forma pauperis* and the accompanying writ of certiorari for justice against the City was also dismissed because of inability to pay court filling fees!

The motion read in part: *...the Clerk is directed not to accept any further petitions in noncriminal matters from petitioner unless the docketing fee required by Rule 38 (a) is paid...* But thanks be to God who cares for the poor orphans and widows docketing fee was provided on the last day of the very month of denial and dismissal for a cry for justice. The $300 is now being provided as certified check in a case the city of Chicago even refused to plead unless compelled by Court.

But a criminal case was lying fallow before your eminent Supreme Court Judges even before the death of the late Associate Justice Antonin Scalia in which petitioner Moore was seeking justice in a Supervision Sentencing – where – Discovery nor specific charge was served Moore before trial which was sudden; legal counsel was not provided by the court to assist and indigent in a criminal case; and even he was not given the option to choose between Jury or Bench trial before Bench Trial was forced on him by retired Hon John Tourtellot of the 4th District Court of Cook, in Illinois – in an unlawful misdemeanor battery trial turn felony prevented a Masters degree holder from working for over 10 years. The case was lying and this court did not consider it.

And when **a political case** came up and was timely filed with court fee paid as enshrined in the *April 2016 Order* to Moore – where he had requested for a re-run Gubernatorial election between the acclaimed winner **Republican Bruce Rauner** and him, **Independent Gregg Moore** for irregularities and injustices encountered in the law at different stages of the electioneering process unto the Judicial hearing of the Illinois Electoral Board resulting his been removed from the ballot – again this court was silent and did nothing.

But when Gubernatorial hopeful came before all you justices of this honorable court about a speedy trial of an election case sitting dormant before it, the United States Supreme Court ruled on a totally different case with **a totally different Case No**. – a criminal case which it allows to be filed free and denied and dismissed it yet cashing the check paid for the political case which it has not ruled upon **until this very moment**. The supposed victim the plaintiff the state backed Rosemary Blair has since dead probably for bearing false with against *another Joseph in "Egypt"* which Moore discovered while seeking Justice, yet justice in that criminal case was denied.

May justice please be done speedily in the case of Moore against the City of Chicago which was dismissed for lack of payment of fees; and also a re-run Gubernatorial Election be ordered in the state of Illinois between acclaimed winner millionaire Bruce Rauner and gubernatorial hopeful marginalized Gregg Moore even though all you 8 judges of the US Supreme Court are Democrats and Republicans and no Independent as petitioner Moore. Thank you

Gregg Moore   3057 West Argyle Street Chicago, IL 60625 (872) 208-5984
Pro Se Petitioner Attorney 99500
1) John G. Roberts, Jr., Chief Justice of the United States
2) Anthony M. Kennedy, Associate Justice,
3) Clarence Thomas, Associate Justice,
4) Ruth Bader Ginsburg, Associate Justice,
5) Stephen G. Breyer, Associate Justice,
6) Samuel Anthony Alito, Jr., Associate Justice,
7) Sonia Sotomayor, Associate Justice,
8) Elena Kagan, Associate Justice, + Scott S. Harris, Clerk, US Supreme Court

THIS CHECK CONTAINS VISIBLE RED & GREEN FIBERS, A VOID BACKGROUND PATTERN AND HAS A TRUE WATERMARK

Credit Union 1

70-8808
2711

VOID AFTER 90 DAYS

Cashier's Check

CHECK NO. **0000086417**

Caballeros de San Juan Branch

200 EAST CHAMPAIGN AVENUE
RANTOUL, IL 61866
(800) 252-6950

DATE
30APR16

AMOUNT
*****$300.00

PAY ■ THREE HUNDRED DOLLARS AND ZERO CENTS **********

PAY
TO THE
ORDER
OF

CLERK US SUPREME COURT***
RE: GREGG ABRAHAM MOORE
GREGG MOORE VS CITY OF CHICAGO

Paul Simms

AUTHORIZED SIGNATURE

⑈0000086417⑈ ⑆271188081⑆0009000600950⑈

Mr. Gregg Moore
3057 W Argyle St
Chicago, IL 60625

CARDO STREAM
IL 605
30 APR '18
PM 10 L

ₕₒₙ SCOTT S. HARRIS
CLERK, SUPREME COURT OF THE UNITED STATE
1 FIRST STREET, NE
WASHINGTON DC 20543

20543

Supreme Court of the United States
Office of the Clerk
Washington, DC 20543-0001

Scott S. Harris
Clerk of the Court
(202) 479-3011

April 4, 2016

Mr. Gregg Moore
3057 West Argyle Street
Chicago, IL 60625

Re: Gregg Moore
v. City of Chicago, Illinois
No. 15-7964

Dear Mr. Moore:

The Court today entered the following order in the above-entitled case:

The motion of petitioner for leave to proceed *in forma pauperis* is denied, and the petition for a writ of certiorari is dismissed. See Rule 39.8. As the petitioner has repeatedly abused this Court's process, the Clerk is directed not to accept any further petitions in noncriminal matters from petitioner unless the docketing fee required by Rule 38(a) is paid and the petition is submitted in compliance with Rule 33.1. See *Martin v. District of Columbia Court of Appeals*, 506 U. S. 1 (1992) (per curiam).

Sincerely,

Scott S. Harris, Clerk

SUPREME COURT
OF THE UNITED STATES

Case Nos.: 15-7964,......

Moore v. City of Chicago	— CIVIL
Moore v. 3 Objectors: Robert I Sherman.. + Illinois Board of Election & Bruce Rauner	— POLITICAL
Moore v. People of the State of Illinois	— CRIMINAL

RECEIVED
MAY ~ 9 2016
OFFICE OF THE CLERK
SUPREME COURT, U.S.

To the entire U S Supreme Court Judges + Clerk of the Court

Earlier this month an order of April 4, 2016 and mailed on April 5, 2016 was received by indigent Pro Se, Petitioner Gregg Moore and signed by Scott S. Harris, Clerk of the court of the denial of petitioner's motion for leave to proceed in *forma pauperis* and the accompanying writ of certiorari for justice against the City was also dismissed because of inability to pay court filling fees!

The motion read in part: *...the Clerk is directed not to accept any further petitions in noncriminal matters from petitioner unless the docketing fee required by Rule 38 (a) is paid...* But thanks be to God who cares for the poor orphans and widows docketing fee was provided on the last day of the very month of denial and dismissal for a cry for justice. The $300 is now being provided as certified check in a case the city of Chicago even refused to plead unless compelled by Court.

But a criminal case was lying fallow before your eminent Supreme Court Judges even before the death of the late Associate Justice Antonin Scalia in which petitioner Moore was seeking justice in a Supervision Sentencing — where — Discovery nor specific charge was served Moore before trial which was sudden; legal counsel was not provided by the court to assist and indigent in a criminal case; and even he was not given the option to choose between Jury or Bench trial before Bench Trial was forced on him by retired Hon John Tourtellot of the 4th District Court of Cook, in Illinois — in an unlawful misdemeanor battery trial turn felony prevented a Masters degree holder from working for over 10 years. The case was lying and this court did not consider it.

And when **a political case** came up and was timely filed with court fee paid as enshrined in the *April 2016 Order* to Moore – where he had requested for a re–run Gubernatorial election between the acclaimed winner **Republican Bruce Rauner** and him, **Independent Gregg Moore** for irregularities and injustices encountered in the law at different stages of the electioneering process unto the Judicial hearing of the Illinois Electoral Board resulting his been removed from the ballot – again this court was silent and did nothing.

But when Gubernatorial hopeful came before all you justices of this honorable court about a speedy trial of an election case sitting dormant before it, the United States Supreme Court ruled on a totally different case with **a totally different Case No.** – a criminal case which it allows to be filed free and denied and dismissed it yet cashing the check paid for the political case which it has not ruled upon **until this very moment**. The supposed victim the plaintiff the state backed Rosemary Blair has since dead probably for bearing false with against *another Joseph in "Egypt"* which Moore discovered while seeking Justice, yet justice in that criminal case was denied.

May justice please be done speedily in the case of Moore against the City of Chicago which was dismissed for lack of payment of fees; and also a re–run Gubernatorial Election be ordered in the state of Illinois between acclaimed winner millionaire Bruce Rauner and gubernatorial hopeful marginalized Gregg Moore even though all you 8 judges of the US Supreme Court are Democrats and Republicans and no Independent as petitioner Moore.

Thank you

Pro Se Petitioner Attorney 99500
1) John G. Roberts, Jr., **Chief Justice of the United States**
2) Anthony M. Kennedy, Associate Justice,
3) Clarence Thomas, Associate Justice,
4) Ruth Bader Ginsburg, Associate Justice,
5) Stephen G. Breyer, Associate Justice,
6) Samuel Anthony Alito, Jr., Associate Justice,
7) Sonia Sotomayor, Associate Justice,
8) Elena Kagan, Associate Justice, + Scott S. Harris, Clerk, US Supreme Court

RESOURCES

Apart from the Holy Bible as source acknowledged in the opening of the work, seven other sources consulted are

1. ABC Chicago Channel 7

2. Fox TV Channel 71

3. NewsDay Reporters News/Media website

4. CNN Channel 50

5. news.yahoo.com/twitter

6. News Express Lagos APC the true face of corruption:Tinubu.. by Ayodele Akele

7. **Premium Times** Tue Jan 12, 2 "Buhari won't probe Tinubu, Fashola because...."

Printed in the United States
By Bookmasters